A Dragonfly lives

Sundari Iyer

BookLeaf Publishing

India | USA | UK

A Dragonfly lives © 2024 Sundari Iyer

All rights reserved.

No part of this publication may be reproduced, stored in a retrieval system, or transmitted, in any form or by any means, electronic, mechanical, photocopying, recording or otherwise, without the prior written permission of the presenters.

Sundari Iyer asserts the moral right to be identified as author of this work.

Presentation by *BookLeaf Publishing*

Web: www.bookleafpub.com

E-mail: info@bookleafpub.com

ISBN: 9789360949051

First edition 2024

To my incredible daughters,

You are my motivation to always be better.
Thank you for being my inspiration, my joy,
and my heart.

ACKNOWLEDGEMENT

This book owes its existence to my daughter, whose insistence that I join her in a writing challenge sparked the journey that led to its creation. What began as a gesture to accompany her transformed into a deeply cathartic exploration of self-discovery and expression.

Thank you, to my brother-in-law Sridhar, whose beautiful painting graces the cover of this book.

PREFACE

Dear Reader,

It is with great pleasure and anticipation that I introduce you to "A Dragonfly Lives," my debut collection of poetry. As I share these verses with you for the first time, I am filled with excitement, gratitude, and a touch of trepidation.

For me, the journey to this moment has been one of introspection, exploration, and discovery. The symbolism of the dragonfly has been a guiding light, illuminating the path as I navigate the twists and turns of life. In these pages, you will find echoes of my experiences, reflections on resilience, and musings on the beauty of transformation.

As you immerse yourself in the words of "A Dragonfly Lives," I hope you will find moments of connection, inspiration, and introspection. May these poems resonate with you, stir your soul, and remind you of the beauty and resilience that reside within each of us.

Thank you for embarking on this inaugural journey with me. May "A Dragonfly Lives" mark the beginning of a meaningful and enriching literary adventure.

With heartfelt gratitude,

Sundari Iyer

Identity

"Good work, now can you do more?"
Atlas picks up the world on his shoulders
Bearing the weight of existence, relentless
"Bad dog, stop that"
Rufus bares his teeth to attack
Instincts primal, a dance of dominance

"Here's your grade, an A"
Jane stops studying, it's too easy
Comfort in competence, complacency thrives
"Here's your grade, an F"
John stops studying, why bother
Apathy takes root, ambition withers

"You topped the list, congratulations"
Lily loses friends to jealousy and resentment
Success, a double-edged sword, cuts deep
"Another lost venture, uh oh
Let's not ask Tom, he doesn't know anything"
Fear of failure, a shadow that looms large

So why do you do what you do
Is it or praise, or perhaps for punishment's
dread?

Do you seek reward, or crave the thrill of
competition
Would you act differently if there was nothing to
gain
Without the fear of loss, or the specter of pain
Would you still tread the same path

Speak the same words, befriend the same souls
Who are you when no one's gaze falls upon you
Would you still stand tall, or crumble in solitude
Would you uphold your values, or surrender
them to the shadows
Would you be your own best companion
Or a stranger even to yourself

Good Girl

Good girl, set the standards high,
Tread the tested, no risks, oh my!
Decisions weighed by what others will say
Heaven forbid a critique come your way
Expected to toe the line, atta girl
Wander off, they think you're just giving it a twirl

Good girl; epitome of sacrifice
Good habits, gracious, no signs of vice
You give you them your umbrella, even in bad weather
You step up to help, you don't know any better
If they hurt you, you brush it aside
Move along to something else, all with a smile

Good girl; what of your hopes and dreams, your aspirations
Did it matter that you wanted to be a dancer, not performing operations
You excelled at school, played sports,
and sang a tune, all while doing chores
People pleaser, you do as they say
You do it for the gratitude they display

Good girl; a paragon of virtue
You do everything right, even if you're dying
inside

Immigrant

I dress like you, I talk like you too
Yearning for a place where I belong, where I'm
true
Work hard to prove, my worth I pursue
Far from home, a journey of rebirth anew

Feeling awkward in this mixed crowd
Seeking familiarity amidst the sound
A phone call from home, a lifeline I seek
Yet their reactions, the words they speak

"Hey, your accent changed," they squeak
Inquiring about customs, assumptions unique
"Aren't your kind supposed to excel in math?"
Other questions that sting, cutting like a swath

"Are women allowed to manage men?"
"Did your parents choose who you'll wed, then?"
"Does your house bear the scent of curry?"
Interrogations that leave me weary

Yet amidst it all, I'm desperate to call this place
home
I find my way, an immigrant in lands not my
own

Despite the color of my skin, home isn't bound
by borders or decree
It's not just where you've been, it's the resilience
and courage within me

Fear

What would you do if fear didn't hold sway
Would you persist on this path, or venture away
Spread your wings wide, risking it all
Conforming, it seems, takes quite the toll
Always wary of misstep and fall
Hesitant, what if you're wrong after all
Fear of stumbling, fear of being wrong
Endless options, yet none feel strong
Is it dread of falling from the pedestal,
Or fear of failure, ridicule, feeling small
What compels such behavior, so deeply
ingrained
Is universal love what you hope to obtain
What's behind this pattern, so hard to sever
Is it fear of slipping from grace forever
Living in the shadows of your own decisions
that were made with so many inhibitions
Potential squandered, you seek validation
Instead of shining brightly, receive crumbs of
appreciation

Without fear, who could you have been
A queen, a goddess, living your dream

Life

I love you
Sometimes I don't like you at all
Weighed down by responsibilities
How will I ever climb
Out of my shell
Explore who I am meant to be
Find time to reflect
Find the real me

They say I solve problems
They love my tales
Should I have been a wordsmith
Instead of climbing corporate trails
An expert at juggling
Without a moment's rest
I feel the stress in my bones
And the muscles as they ache

I have miles to go
Dreams to bring alive
I don't want to drown
Working a nine to five
Take a day off to play
Smell the roses, feel the rain
Today's little detour
Will be tomorrow's gain

Being Present

My mind races ahead
A million different things -
Pots bubbling on the stove
Laundry piles ready to fold
Dishes in the sink waiting to be cleaned
Dogs barking, eager to be fed
Kids running wild, needing to be reined
Lessons to plan, feeling strained
Miles to run, paths to be braved
Songs to sing, spirits to be saved
Events to attend, friends to meet
Old family to love, new members to greet
Calls to make, voices to hear
Bills to pay, goals to steer

What will it take to stay awake
To cherish the present for goodness sake
Calm the chaos, take a deep breath in
And in that moment, fall in love again …

Mistakes

Silly
Costly
Covered up
Exposed
Embarrassed
Inconsequential
Life-changing

Does it haunt you?
Do you live in regret?
Does it define you?
Did it ruin you?

What's done is done
Do you
Atone?
Brush it off?
Compensate?
Lie?

Learning only happens from
The mistakes you survive

Jaded

I met you at sixteen
We should be friends
You pursued and persisted
Friends make the best partners
Ten years later

I fell in love…

Got married
Moved to the other side of the world
Made a home
Made babies
Made money
Bought houses
Hosted parties
Traveled the world

I thrived…

You harbored resentment
Life with me became mundane
You craved excitement
I settled for stability and staying sane
We drifted apart
Couldn't find our way back

I felt my soul crumble…

I said, "I'm done"
Your resentment grew fiercer
Breaking us shattered your trust
I should've persevered, but I didn't know how
I try with others, but it never lasts
None of them are you
It took ten years to fall in love
How many more will it take to fall out

I'm broken…

Take the Time to Mourn

A cheery smile
Hiding the pain inside
Faking happy
Avoiding questions
Being what you expect me to be

I just need a little time
To mourn
Loss of a friendship
End of a relationship
Failure of an endeavor
Death of a loved one
Passing of beauty with time
Flaws of human nature
Betrayal of someone close
Unpredictability of an outcome

Sometimes things are
sad, unexpected, undesired
But they happen anyway
To truly live
I need to feel
the good, the bad, and the ugly
Experience the darkness
to appreciate the light

Purge

Mattresses laid out on the floor
The old beds are gone, the couches too
Spoons, plates, chairs, and tables
desperate to wipe all traces of you
If I could move, I would
Put this house and its stories behind
Unfettered by memories, good and bad
A fresh start to ease my mind

New furniture for a new me
Out with the old, in with the new
New drapes, its has dragonflies
Changed the walls from yellow to blue
A new tribe from same old friends
No more heels, hello Converse
Embrace the job that's more than a distraction
Cheers to colleagues, and happy hours

I changed my social circle
I changed my home decor
Anything that we had as the two of us
I replaced, it exists no more
Is that enough to stop the hurt
Is that enough to open new doors
Who will I be when the dust clears
A heart still healing, or a dragonfly that veers

Bad Decisions

Sad movies make me cry
Happy endings too
I see the hero jump through hoops
But none of those moves end in "oops"
What is it about my choices
that make even simple tasks look like vices
No, I'm not making this up
Here's the list straight from the top

Men in my books hold their women on a
pedestal
I end up with those who leave me unsettled
Everyone I hire makes it to the top
Here I am standing, holding straws in an empty
cup
Good wives are good housekeepers, project
managers and lovers
Yet I was the one who was boring and dull, my
life going in reverse
Life of the party, they all want to be my friend
When I'm in trouble, there's no one at this end
I start my own business, master of my own time
My friends are now CEOs, I'm scraping for each
dime

The list may lengthen, but its weight holds no
sway
For when life serves lemons, I'll make lemonade
With each misstep, life takes its own twist,
Yet the dragonfly whispers: adapt, persist
No single savior shall come to my aid
Yet with my tribe, I'll stand unswayed
Though I may stumble, shed tears on my way
Like the dragonfly, I'll evolve, come what may

Letting Go

I gave you my heart, my trust, my soul
You shattered it, leaving me in a hole
Once, we knew each other inside out
Or maybe we didn't, how do I move on without
a doubt

We lost our way, couldn't find our track
But it's alright, even the best veer off the path
Must we turn to hate, to inflict pain
Or can we part ways with grace, and not disdain

Being mean and spiteful, that's quite a chore
Instead, let's choose kindness, and shut the door
For in the end, it's not about the fight
But how we choose to move towards the light

Lawyers, counselors, their pockets filled with
gold
Kids, in need of healing, their stories yet untold
They're your children too, where's your shelter
in the rain
They bear the wounds, while I emerge unscathed

How long will this linger, spiteful years a weary
strain

Once promised amicable, now fraught with pain
Life partners no more, our paths have diverged
Yet can't we restore civility, purpose converged

It's Okay

I have much to do today
dirty dishes and baskets of laundry
untidy home, at least it's clean
Boss's email
something was due yesterday
Kids' report without all As
The pressure on myself
to be a wonderful housekeeper
A hardworking employee, and raising
overachievers
Let them be
it's okay

On my deathbed
my fondest memories
Will be with loved ones
Holiday movie binges, impromptu fashion
shows
Birthday dinners, cooking disasters
Stolen clothes from my closet
Words and feelings whispered in secret
Trips taken, music in the park
Happy clients and colleagues, now friends
Precious memories
Only for me

it's okay

Dreams that became reality
Unexpected turns that
strengthened the body and soul
Friends, family, acquaintances, strangers
Joy of interaction
love, hate, and everything in between
disappointment, introspection
mistakes repeated, lessons learned
Feeling everything, missing nothing
Worn pages of a often-read book
A life well lived
it's okay

Dating

Venturing into the realm of dating, unfamiliar
and vast
Encountering ghosts, bots, and scammers,
emotional baggage with a past
One side leaves, the other is left in the dark
It's a messed up game, truth's like hitting a spark
Don't even get me started on the crazy and
bizarre
Real men no doubt, but that'll probably leave a
scar

I keep pushing forward, these wild and bumpy
roads
Friends cheer me on, laughing at the toads
Did you hear of my latest disaster
At social engagements, its a real conversation
starter
I find myself wanting to get off this crazy train
Stop the cycle of hope from playing a mind
game

In the wake of heartbreak, the urge to step back
Pretend I'm fine alone, keep my life on track
I wake up with gratitude for a life so bright

I look forward to everyday, living healthy and
eating right
Kids, dogs, family, friends, they're all part of my
sphere
But is it wrong to want more, someone to hold
dear

Strangers

Meet __, he has five daughters
I have three so we should be friends
Talking, laughing, singing
Is he flirting with me?
Silence…

He's married
My wife is my Northstar
I can't help myself
We can't do this
Silence …

Hello, is this still your number?
Together, like we were never apart
But he's still married
We can't do this
Silence …

Hello, did you know my husband
He says you pursued him
You're a slut, leave him alone
I never had him, he was always yours
We never did this
Silence …

Stillness

A noisy mind reacts
A quiet mind reflects
An idle mind creates
with potential unchecked

So react
until a habit's firmly instilled
Reflect on your actions
till their purpose fulfilled

Create your future self
from quiet contemplation
Let your thoughts guide
like the stars in a constellation

Be quiet
yet be heard in your silence profound
In the stillness of your soul
wisdom will be found

Faith

"You are supposed to have the answers to
everything"
"You always help anyone unconditionally
understanding"
"You're smart enough to land on your feet and
thrive"
"You'll be successful wherever you go, you've
got the drive"
"You can't go wrong when you trust your
instincts"
"When I grow up, I'll follow your footprints"
"You intimidate me, your confidence shines"
"I'll have what she has, what's hers is mine"

What do they see in me that I don't
What truths do they perceive, while I remain in
want
When I look in the mirror, that's not who I see
Survival instincts don't translate to glory

The imposter laughs. I've done well.
I've done my job; look, they can't even tell
Shhh.. says the brain. Manifestation is real, I'll
prove
when the soul starts to believe, she'll make it
come true

Woman

You don't need a cape
(though you'd totally rock that shape)
Birthing a human's no joke
You've got the power, no need to cloak
You do you, I'll do me
Let's live and let be
Don't stand in my way, you'll see
I've earned my freedom, I'm living free

Mother, sister, daughter, lover
Coworker, manager, teacher, business owner
Singer, writer, runner, knitter
Acquaintance, friend, ally, foe
So many hats, what do you know
Don't let them define you, don't let them say
This is your lane
This is where you'll stay

Frustrating, overwhelming, motivating,
exhilarating
Success, failure, wounds, heartaches
Pick up again, here we go
The only wrong answer - don't say no
Chances not taken
is life not lived

Tried and tested
Some wholesome, some wasted

A woman, I stand proud and strong
I too was a girl once, unsure of myself, so wrong
They told me I couldn't and so I did
My mistakes were mine, but the successes are
big
When you grow up will you aspire to be me
No vanity here, just the person I hope to be
So don that cape, if it lifts your mood
Embrace it, woman, that's how the world's
viewed

It's Not Fair

"It's not fair"
That's a common refrain
No it isn't
But whining has no gain

Fairness is a mirage
An intricate scheme
Where one side triumphs
And the other can't dream

Today may not favor you
But tomorrow who's to say
Life is askew
A truth that cannot sway

The dice is loaded
That much is true
Learn the rules
And see them through

Take the punches
Forge your own way
Survival of the fittest
Play or be played

Call me cynical
Call me a skeptic
When everyone's winning
It's hard not to be a critic

If karma's real
Let it unfold
I'll sit back and watch
See what the future holds

Justice must prevail
Even if not for me
Restore my faith
In life's grand decree

A Noisy Mind

I can't bring myself to do nothing
Stare into space and dream
Sing along to a record
Indulge in cake and ice cream
Is going for a walk is a waste of time
Unless I walk the dogs as well
Can I read a book about witches and faeries
Without learning something in parallel

When did my life become this way
Tasks completed, I measure my day
The mind guilts me from taking a break
unless its a family vacation or a weekend
getaway
Should everything have a purpose
Why not just be
Live in the moment. Do something
that means something only to me

Good morning, today is a new day
I slowly sip my tea
I look out through my window
The sun is rising above the trees
The day can wait
God knows it'll cause quite a stir

Kids, dogs, work, chores
There's plenty to be running after

I'm going to cherish this moment
The calm before the storm
Even the dogs are asleep
This quiet is my time
Focus on the mug that keeps my hands warm
Not think about to-do lists, no plans, no strategy
This moment right here right now
I don't owe anything, not even to me

A Dragonfly Lives

Born in water, alive in the breeze
Symbol of resilience, joy, and ease
A link to the spirit world unfurled
Time for transformation, let those wings swirl
I was drawn to them, a chosen few
When chaos reigned, but skies were blue
How nice it would be to be carefree
To ignore the world, and simply be
They love the rain with a fiery passion
Change course without skipping a fraction
That's the strength I yearn to grasp
To face life's trials, no matter the task

A dragonfly lives, in flight it thrives
Speed, grace, in playful dives
Stay lighthearted, let your soul stroll
Navigate life's waves at every toll
Swoop in, be saved, your spirit revived
By yourself, in freedom, rejoice
You have it within, just believe
in your wings, the power to achieve
Don't question fate, don't let hate inflate
What's meant to be will resonate
Be like the dragonfly, take to the sky
Let your spirit soar, don't ask why

www.ingramcontent.com/pod-product-compliance
Lightning Source LLC
LaVergne TN
LVHW010925200726

843509LV00013B/2086